It's a new day and as I sit and write, I have to wonder about nothing because there is nothing to wonder about.

I can only listen to music and hope that these songs ease my pain.

Hope that tomorrow and today become good and be in my favour.

Yes I need a vacation
I need a good and true blessing because my body is tired and in need of rest.

Man does it need rest but I have to wait until my time comes for me to jet away.

I truly hope soon because I don't know how much I can take.

I need blessings
Anointing

I need to wash me
Wash away my sins.

Michelle Jean

I need to be me
Need the forces of good to surround me
Need to find me

No, not find me because I am no longer lost. I know me just need to get rid of the negative energy that surrounds me.

I do not need to be found just need something different in my life.

If only the goodness of Good God's abode could open up to me all at once and shower me with all that is good and true - honest and clean.

Ah well. It's good to wonder and ponder but then again is that not me.

Me wanting to do something different for a change.

Yes I want and need to create but when will the time come?

When will I create those sexy clothes that I so need to create.

No, I don't want to create old clothes but new clothes. Sexy clothes for the voluptuous woman. Women like me.

Michelle Jean

It's October 09, 2013 and on this day I so do not need pictures in this book.

I want and need it to be picture free.

Don't know where I am going with this hence I should start doing something with my old stuff.

Yes my old writings I want and need to put in a book entitled Michelle Jean the early years. No not old days because I am not ancient. I am aged but not ancient.

I guess it's me because as of late I've been buying old people clothing which makes me feel old.

I guess I am in the old phase where I've become old. My spirit is no longer young and vibrant. It feels old hence I'm acting old and dressing old.

I need my spirit to be stimulated but that stimulation I do not know how to get. No, I so do not want to live a cougar lifestyle where I find a young turbine for my rucumbine. Don't need a young stud that just comes.

Need the brain to be stimulated the right and proper way because in my book a young buck – stud is just a stud. Can't fulfill me.

Yes people there is more to my world than sex.

I truly love to shop but shop where?

Maybe one day Ryan Seacrest and I will go shopping together. He would be my perfect shopping buddy.

I truly love to give and it's not all that I give to.

Yes I am stuck in my ways, hence the young bucks and studs are not on my list because when it comes to sex, they have nothing to give me apart for their vitamin S and that I so do not need every day.

Yes sex is boring hence my body only need it when it needs it.

Michelle Jean

The life of man is not secure because
his end is near.

The rich man will die like the poor man
He will die alone
Die for want
Die for and of need

In all the rich man did he never thought
of the consequences of tomorrow.

In all he did, he did to kill
Control
Dominate
Enslave

His need is wealth
Having it all
Staying atop of the game
Forging ahead and forgetting about
tomorrow; the consequences of his
actions.

He never thought of preservation
Replenishing what he took to save
tomorrow.

Ah yes in all he gained he lost
Will die for want and need.

Michelle Jean

How can God – Good God have mercy on the wicked when all they do is try to destroy the earth and control humanity including kill the innocent of the world including land.

In all that evil do and does Good God would never give them power to continue to kill. He must take their power away this I infinitely know.

He Good God must return their sins back to them (sender). Hence hell awaits all wicked and evil man including children.

Many muse and say there is no hell but what a pity they don't know the truth.

What a pity they do not know their end because if they did, many things they do on earth they would not do.

Ah as Bob Marley says, Time Will Tell. When you think you're living in heaven you're living in hell and he is so correct.

Michelle Jean

This is my day and I so do not know what to think of it because it's early morning and I so can't go back to sleep.

Too much to do and it seem like housework can never finish.

It seem like I am a slave to others. I'm not fed up of helping but when do you stop?

Do I even want to stop helping others?

I say not but it does become tiring — taxing on your body because you have to do all and all can never be done or get done.

The constant cleaning is what I so don't like because the more you clean it's the dirtier your place gets.

Yes I have to do it all but would I change the goodness in my heart? I say not because you do not think about financial constraints just the hardships of doing it all. And this is not all the time. You make do with what you have until better comes — you can do better.

Yes its hard work but what can you do?

Good is what you truly love and goodness you must do?

For me when I help, I am expecting the person to get ahead – move ahead in life in a positive and good way.

It means you're to pay down your bills if you are working because I am taking some of the financial burdens off you.

I'm taking some of the stress off you.

What you need to do to help you, you are to do. If you do not do what you need to do to truly help you then that would mean the help I give was in vain. You did not truly love you or care about you.   .

I've burdened myself to help you and burdened is not the right word but it's the only word I had to use.

Michelle Jean

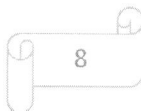

My Day is my day and I am getting stressed.

Its 1:37 AM in the morning and trust me I never knew puppies were this demanding and taxing on the body.

Wow.

I don't know how much more I can take of this without snapping because my nights are filled with so much noise. While the owner sleeps my nights are sleepless because these puppies are so demanding.

The noise at feeding time is unbelievable. Man the puppies are feeding and they are making the most noise as if they are hungry. They are on the breast feeding and still making noise. Man you should see them on the breast. They are getting full enjoyment but the noise drives you crazy.

You cannot sleep. Man taking care of them is like taking care of human babies with the exception you get more noise. I don't think I could go through this again because stress level goes up.

Michelle Jean

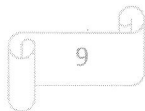

I so need to do something with self.

Need a change in my life and hopefully 2014 see true and positive changes in my life.

I need to come out of the darkness of the night because the darkness of the night is not helping me. Nor is it helping this world.

I don't know but this morning I have to wonder why we believe in God?

Why we put our trust in him when the world stinks to high hell.

Everything is based on domination and lies. Corruption of men – evil men that dictate your life at will.

Corrupt men and women that sell you lies while their pocket book become full with greed.

It matters not to me anymore because each and every day I get disappointed in God – Good God because humans cut down the trees at will just to sell disaster – fill their greedy bellies.

In all the development of man, none has thought of the trees – preserving their future.

All we want we take and destroy in the process of taking it all.

We give no thought to the environment. We give no thought to the eroding soil of earth.

We give no thought of the future of our children – future generations.

We give no thought of our own greed. We give no thought to the manipulative systems of earth because all we do, we design to destroy and kill.

We kill the trees now tell me how are we going to replenish the earth if there are no seeds and seedlings to replenish earth with?

Earth is becoming a dying planet. She did not cause this. Humans caused her to die because humans take at will and destroy in the process of taking.

No one thought of earth's children – the trees and water including the good food of this earth.

We care not to clean up the earth hence we dump all in her and expect someone else to fix and or repair the damage we've done.

Yes I look forward to the day when man – humanity will have no clean drinking water and food to eat.

No for real people. I truly look forward to the day when lands become barren – void of food and water.

We killed earth and in the process of killing earth we killed self. Will become extinct and I so love it because humans – humanity have and has become the height of all things evil.

Like I said, we think of self without thought of the environment we live in. We over populate the land and think we are good to go. We did not think that trees are a part of life because they help to maintain and sustain us.

Because of greed – the greed of men – humanity we've dug a pit and cannot get out of this pit hence we talk about hell. Shortly man will face hell on earth. Many will more than cry and die. Hell awaits us all and shortly hell's belly will be fed with the spiritual lives of billions.

Billions that cared not about earth because we pollute at will.

Create garbage at will
Dirtied the planet at will
Polluted the water of earth at will

Destroy and kill the trees of earth at will

Destroy and kill the resources of earth at will

All these things we did at will hence willful sins are not forgiven.

Willful sins go against God – Good God hence many are slated to die. Yes the judgement of many will be severe but this is what humanity wanted and needed. We've proven to self and God that we cannot live without him. We are like unto dogs because we are beggars unto him.

All he's given us we've destroyed including destroying self. We destroy self but cannot stop the destruction we are doing to self.

We think as long as we get it today we do not have worry about tomorrow because we have a sacrificial lamb. Meaning someone will come along and fix our mess. But in reality someone can fix what you have done. You have to fix your problem and that problem is you.

You cannot expect someone to fix your mess hence humanity and or society is the way they are.

Men create mess
Men create diseases
Men created death
Men create pollution
Men create problems
Men create ghettos
Sins

All that you see around us man created but yet none can see this. We make mess and instead of cleaning up the mess we made we put more mess on top of mess hence accumulating more mess.

We've become people of mess hence we are messy and know not how to clean earth and self.

We hide our mess in the earth and water hence making the planet stinky – void of its natural scent.

Earth has lost her fragrance because the stench we accumulate along with cutting down the cedar trees amongst others. Now Earth is left with the stench of human waste not just in her but also above her. Yes our stench has and have become air borne.

We also allow others to put us into more mess and instead of coming out of it we wallow in it like pigs.

It seems like we love mess. So the mess we keep in our homes and self, we take it outside and pollute the earth and others with it.

We've accumulated so much filth that we can't even swim in some of our lakes and seas because of human feces – waste. Not to mention the chemical toxins we dump in our eco system - waterways.

When all of this crap – shit starts to stink we start complaining and say the government isn't doing anything. But look into it. Did the government dump these crap into the system or did you the consumer. Are we not the ones to buy foods filled with chemicals?

Are we not the ones to buy cars that use toxins to run them?

So are we not the contributor to the problem of the eco system?

Are we as consumers not the ones to contribute to global warming?

Come on think about it. If we do not buy gas and buy biodegradable fuel that do not harm the environment, can the ozone deplete?

If we bought clean fuel that is made from plant based products, can we contribute to the depletion of the ozone?

If we made solar cars that uses no fluids, can we deplete the water or contribute to the depletion of the ozone?

Like I said, we destroy as well as contribute to the problem of the earth and instead of cutting back on the garbage we put in our landfills we add more to it.

Instead of adding more garbage to the landfills why not build incinerators and start burning some of the garbage we store up in landfills. If our garbage cannot be incinerated then find other means of getting rid of it.

My idea is to dump some of our garbage into active volcanoes but that's just me and my whacked out ideas.

Like I said, my brain does not function like the rest of humanity because I so do not think inside the box. My thoughts are outside the box hence the universe is mine. If my brain can find a way to get to the universe and preserve it then yes I would.

Yes the black hole is mine but I've yet to see inside of them or explore them. Maybe later on in life but for now I will let nature take its course because I know shortly, humanity will become extinct. And like I said, it would be well deserved because humanity seek to destroy and kill then lay the blame on evil – Satan when we are the evil ones.

We are the creators of evil not God or Satan.

We have the tools of sin hence we willingly use these tools to destroy planet and self.

We destroy all around us now we say we are going into space to destroy that too.

Wow.

What a lala when gravity decides it will not aide man – humanity by keeping the earth up!

What a lala when gravity say, screw earth and humanity. I am taking away my services hence let humanity and earth crumble.

What a lala when gravity say, shit just for the heck of it I am going to change my polarity and pull as many asteroids to earth so that they can do their damage. Like destroy man at least what will be left of man after the harvest has and have taken fold.

What a lala when gravity stop laughing at man and get serious.

Yes man – humanity does not know the seriousness of their wickedness hence the extinction of the wicked and evil real soon.

In all we do we blame Satan but truly tell me this, how can we blame Satan for what we did?

No, nó, no don't go there because I know we can blame him for many things. But in truth can we truly blame Satan or Sin for our wrongs? What we do to self and others including Good God and the planet earth?

Did Satan or Sin commit these wrongs or did you?

Did Satan and Sin commit my wrongs so truly how can I or you blame someone else for the sins WE AS A PERSON DO AND DID?

We sinned
We did wrong

So how can I blame the next man for what I did?

Are we not the true destroyers of the planet earth?

Now tell me this. Are we not the true children of Adam and Eve?

Did they not blame someone else for their wrongs?

Did they get away with it?

No right?

So how are you going to get away with it?

Adam and Eve knew right from wrong hence they were punished.

She Eve broke the code of Good God because she laid with a deceiver and he did deceive. Today we are no different. I'm no different from you because I've done the same thing.

Hence we know not God and the goodness of him.

I know many of us are saying we are redeemed because one died for our sins and we are to wash in the blood of the lamb.

We are to be sacrifices onto him because he did sacrifice himself for us.

And like I've said time and time again, Jesus did not exist nor will he exist.

Infinitely know that Good God would infinitely never ever send anyone to die for your sins. **Your sins are your sins and not the next man's. You erred hence he cannot take your sins. Your sins are recorded in your book of records and it will remain in your book of records until the flesh dies.**

Once the flesh dies and it is brought back into the darkness of the night, you will know your faith; meaning which way your eye in the triangle goes. If it goes down, know that you are going down to hell and if it goes up, you are going up to see Good God. This is the reality and truth of man – humanity hence no one can or will die for your sins.

Also, death will never accept one man or an individual's death for the sins of humanity. Infinitely never ever going to happen. Impossible, hence death bank our sins. Death's bank account is more than full with the sins of man. *Hence he has you in his bank honey and collecting interest on you.* See the more you sin is the longer you stay in the underworld or grave with him (death and the demons of hell).

So yes I can safely say on my day, which is this day death has more money in his bank account than Good God.

Count up the sins of man – humanity compared to the good of man – humanity.

But my goodness can wipe out thousands of sins you are saying.

True but is your goodness truly good?

Like I said, we cannot do to get. We have to be true to good and the goodness that we do. **If you do to get you will never get into Good God's abode.** Good God do not do to get anything from you. He do and does because he loves us so. We need his goodness because without his goodness we cannot survive. And yes this is why the world – earth and people are this way today.

We've separated ourselves from God. Many of us have also divorced him. So because we've separated ourselves from him as well as divorced him you find, no not find you see that we cannot survive nor can we do without him. A prime example of this is the disarray that the world is in today. Instead of preserving goodness we destroy it. Instead of preserving life we destroy life – kill life.

Instead of living to live we live to die.

So in all that we do we do no good. We do all that is evil hence we are farther away from God than our ancestors were.

We do not thrive on goodness, we thrive on evil – the bad things we can create and do create.

Today lies have and has become the foundation of man – humanity because we live by lies hence lies dictate our lives as well as dominate and control it.

Truth have no merit with man anymore because we made earth the domain and kingdom of lies and wickedness.

No other universe is based on lies. Yes the planet of death.....no I can't say that because in all I saw with these three people, it was not lies that they brought but death. Hence true death, the

death of spirit lies on another planet –
domain. ***True death is not on earth but
in hell and hell is truly not on earth.***

This planet – the domain of the dead
wow. And I am truly going to leave this
alone because dead bodies no longer
scare me.

To me the scariest part of death is the
draining of the blood from the body.
This is sickening and gross and in truth
this should never be.

***Human blood should not be drained from
the body. This is wrong in my book.*** Yes
the spirit hath nothing to do with blood
but blood is a part of the flesh hence
the body needs it. The blood is the fuel
because without this fuel our bodies
cannot function.

*Blood is a part of physical time for
women because like I've said, women are
the true keepers of time. We tell time
every 28 days hence one cycle of life
which is the square. And this analogy is
wrong because a woman have more than 12
periods in one year. Hence one year is
13 months plus a day.*

Yes this is weird for some but I care not about the weirdness because this is reality, the truth.

Evil fears 13. Hence evil tries to omit this because everything to do with evil hath to do with 12 - halves but there are no halves with Good God. Good God can only deal with the full cycle of things. He does not give you things in halves he gives them to you in full hence we cannot go hungry when it comes to Good God. Evil keep us hungry and fighting all the time and this is due to the greed of man. Every leader want to dominate and control - have it all but this cannot be because Good God told no one to control each other or the next person.

13 is the birthday of God - Good God hence 13 hath to do with good life. Yes the mountain of good life and truth for those who use the mountain analogy.

Furthermore, in regards to domination and control we are to blame because it seems like we like to be dominated and controlled. If we didn't, we would not have evil people governing us globally.

As individuals we need to care about our lives as well as well being. If you don't, then you are lost in the cold and dark. Your soul or spirit is essential hence you are to protect it from all evil.

Yes we want to gain but what is the point of gaining if we have nothing. Meaning someone else is governing us and telling us what we can and cannot do. As long as you are truthful to self and God – Good God and you are not breaking the laws of man and God then you are good to go.

No one should come and tell you God does not like this or that if they are not ordained by Good God to do so.

No one should come and tell you that you are not going to reach Good God's abode if you are living true and clean with Good God.

No one should come and tell you that Good God does not like you if they are not ordained by Good God to do so.

No one should come and tell you, you are going to hell and burn if you do not accept Christ – their false and deceitful god. Good God did not give humanity or anyone the Christ or Jesus because all of Good God's children are females. Females are the messengers of Good God and this is because Good God is female in the physical realm. Males have a role to play yes but you have to know the spiritual realm to know. Yes Good God gives you things directly but the role of males are of protection and nothing else from what I've seen. Males are the protector for the female messengers. This is what I see and how I see it hence there could never have been a Christos – male child of Good God.

No one should come and tell you that Good God's abode houses streets of gold when they have never set foot in Good God's abode.

Remember no fleshy can get into Good God's abode if we stink, tell lies and live in sin on a daily basis.

No one should come and tell you this or that when they are not ordained by Good God to do so.

No one should come and tell you anything when they themselves cannot tell you what Good God like from what he does not like if he Good God has not told that person to do so.

I cannot comprehend why WE WANT TO BELONG WHEN WE KNOW NOT WHAT TO BELONG TO OR WHAT WE WANT TO BELONG TO.

Because of this we've become confused and disoriented. Nowadays it seems that we all know Good God and can speak for him when we know him not nor can speak for him. In so doing, I do not blame certain members of society to say there is no God hence they don't believe in him.

They are not wrong in saying this because the god we are given is not the right God.

The god that is being shoved down our throats by the clergy is not the right god. The clergy sells death hence the god you believe in and worship is death hence death takes us.

We willingly hand over our lives to death and we are okay with this.

This is what we believe so no one should blame Good God for disappointing them. He Good God did not disappoint you, you disappointed self because you willingly buy dead and hand over your life unto death.

Eve chose death and she died but before she died she had to feel pain – the pain of death. It did not work out for her and it will not work out for you either.

There are 3 deaths and the final death is brutal. ***I've told you it is not the flesh that feels pain it is the spirit.***

<u>The spirit is the one to leave the flesh not the other way around.</u> *So you need to know what you are doing because at the end of the day if you are not living right you are going to die. No one can change this not even Good God himself.*

Like I've said, we are accountable for our actions and no one is going to burn in hell for you – your sins.

I wouldn't.

I wouldn't burn in hell for Good God either.

Yes I truly love him but certain sacrifices I refuse to make and will not make them because right is right and wrong is wrong. I will not give my soul or spirit as a sacrifice for anyone not even Good God. Yes mistakes are made and it is up to us to correct ourselves and not make those mistakes again and again.

And for those that are saying you didn't truly love Good God if you are not willing to burn in hell or give up your soul or spirit for him. To you I say it is a foolish man or woman that think this way or would go to hell and burn for the next man or god.

**True love cannot sacrifice anything because true love is true. There is no dying in truth but life. Hence no one can sacrifice self for truth or true love – the true love of God – Good God.**

**This is why I tell you God – Good God would never let any of his messengers die for anyone.**

**Death is not a part of the portfolio of Good God. Death is a part of the portfolio of sin. Sin is death's stock market. This stock market never declines. Death's stock will forever rise hence death has no profit or loss statements.**

Death has no balance sheet because death's toll will always rise. Can never decline given the present state of man – humanity and the sins that we commit.

This is why I tell you death's bank account is fat and full. Death has more money than Good God. And no one can dispute this. All Death and Good God have to do is look at each other's bank account meaning your record of good and evil. Hence death has and have Good God beat by more than a long shot when it comes to monetary gain.

Many of you are saying, no death does not and I am telling you death does. **See death's money is your soul or spirit.** Death owes you nothing but you as a person owe death hence I've told you time and time again "the wages of sin is death." Hence your sins are death's pay. Death insurance policy that he must get paid hence death can never be loyal to anyone or anything a part from death.

When you give your soul or spirit over to death good luck in getting it back because there are no givesy backsy when it comes to death and I've told you this.

But but but.

No buts. Your clergy willingly hand you over to death hence hell is full of black people and recruiting more. Sin and death have and has their own people hence sin and death are not worried about them. They are infinitely and indefinitely locked in hell already and no one can take them out if they are not commissioned to do so by Good God. And like I said, Good God does not deal in unclean, he only deals in clean. Hell is unclean hence death's children live there. *God's children cannot go to hell or into hell and take you out just like that. If they did they too would become unclean. Hence when the church tell me and you someone died for our sins and everything will be okay I say good luck with that. Truly good luck because I know otherwise. I know death and what death is capable of. Death do not like to lose so truly good luck with your soul and or spirit in the grave.*

You are accountable for your sins and this is why the dead cries when they enter the grave.

This is also why the dead cry out to the living and say water is coming in on them.

This is also why people see spirits amongst the living because those spirits have and has no resting place.

The spiritual realm is no different from the physical realm and this is why you are told as it is in heaven so it is on earth.

So because there are spiritual wickedness in high and low places Good God cannot reside in the spiritual realm. Hence I do not strive to be amongst the physical or spiritual wicked. I strive to be amongst Good God in his abode which is not the spiritual realm.

And no the spiritual realm is not a transition state. The spiritual realm is where evil dies. I've told you and shown you the planet of spiritual evil. This planet has access to the earth and this is because of our sins.

We sin hence we accept sin and all the negative energy sin has to offer. Like I said, death is richer than God — Good

God because of us - humanity and our sins.

We are the cause of this rift - negative energy and force.

Like I said, if we sin not death would not come.

If the government of the world stopped killing then death would not come persay. Meaning if your country stopped killing or going to war to fight another man's battle your land and people would not be indebted to death. Your country would not owe death then.

The instability of your economy would become stable if that sounds right. Your country would not be in financial ruin then.

THOU SHALT NOT KILL for those who went there. And yes I rushed to type those words before you could say it.

Don't even go there because I know before you even say it.

It's not impossible hence I would not write it.

Like I've said, we are to live clean and void of sin.

Living clean becomes easier as you clean yourself up. But living void of sin is next to impossible because we live amongst sinful and wicked people. If we did not live amongst sinful and wicked people then things would be different.

Also note: the food that we eat also plays an important part in our lives. Certain foods we are not to eat nor are we to consume chemically induced foods. I know this is hard because virtually everything we eat has some form of chemical in it. Hence I will promote 100% organic foods, foods void of chemicals and fertilizers; chemicals and fertilizers that harm our body including our DNA.

I know many will argue this argument hence the world is over populated and soon man – humanity will become extinct.

Once this happens spiritual life for many will become extinct as well. Like I've said, the flesh is the conductor for the body on earth. Once the spirit sheds the flesh – body then it moves up

or down depending on your way of life.
Religion also plays a factor in this.

Because we sell ourselves in regards to religion and it matters not what sect of religion you follow, you are going to die. Hence billions are on the chopping block meaning your name is in death's book and you are going to die.

God – Good God is not a religion and I've told you this. We all say religion can get us into the abode or kingdom of God and I've asked if so, which religion is God or does God practice? What religious denomination is Good God or God?

No one on the face of this planet can tell you but yet everyone say they know him and is practicing his religion.

I will repeat. Good God is not a religion and to say you are from this religious denomination you are wrong. You are sinning hence in the end Good God or God will not look upon you because you lied. You lived your life in a lie.

No messenger can say they are from this or that religion because Good God never

gave them a religious denomination to belong to. Impossible, hence Good God has no religion or religious beliefs.

He gives us knowledge and one of his knowledge is cleanliness and truth. Truth is everlasting life hence we are to live honest, good and true at all times. Without these three things you cannot see him nor enter his kingdom.

Good God never said worship me. **The message on the school wall read, "FOR GOD SO LOVE US HE IS WORTHY TO BE PRAISED."** Praise does not mean worship, it means thanks. We are to thank him for the goodness he has given us.

It is simple courtesy people. When someone do good unto us, do we not thank them? So what makes God – Good God any different? He does good for us each and every day so give him thanks.

Well I'm unemployed and he's not helping me to find a job.

Have you ever tried networking?

Nowadays if you do not network you can't get anywhere. It's all about network but where to start is another chapter. Try

LinkedIn or a recruiting agency that caters to your specific needs meaning qualifications. ***And don't stay stuck in one area. Many of us are not willing to relocate. If you can relocate then relocate. Your life does not revolve around one area. The earth is vast so utilize it.*** Trust me if given the opportunity to relocate, I would be outta here before you can say Jesus wept. I don't want to be stuck in an area that brings me pure unhappiness. I need to be in a place where I can find happiness and be happy. ***Take that rural job if that makes you happy but make sure that job can support you and your family if you have a family.***

It's amazing how we all want to be stuck in the city. God how a truly hate the city. Too much damned vehicle, people and noise not to mention pollution. Who wants that? Keep the damned city life and give me the country any day. City life is too damned stressful but country life is bliss – more than golden.

Yes this is my day and I can speak my mind and do what I want to. But today things are truly different. Don't want to speak my mind because there is nothing on my mind that I want to truly speak about.

Troubles are real and it seem like my problems cannot stop. Wow. But I won't get into it because problems come and go but mine seem to constantly stay.

So on this day I am going to endorse these songs:

My Day	*Tarrus Riley*
Better Way	*Jah Cure*
It's Not Right	*Demarco*
Anything's Possible	*Tessanne Chin*

Truly listen to **_It's Not Right by Demarco_** because this is reality. The day to day life of Jamaican children and the scum bags in the government of Jamaica turn a blind eye to it. Listen to what he said if this happened to his kids. ***Trust me I do not blame him because the slackness and nastiness must stop. Pedophiles run free in Jamaica because grown ass men prey on the children and no one is frigging doing anything about it.***

All we can do is sing and no one is taking heed. ***Trust me the F***ing Jamaican Government should be hung by*** *their dicks and clits because they condone slackness. The willful rape and murder of young kids – children.*

Grown ass men should not be F***ing children. Come on now. Father's raping their own children and slaughtering them like pigs and nothing is done. Come on now. This is not life it's bullshit.

Like I've said, the world tribunal only look at certain things but yet children are being slaughtered daily in Jamaica and they turn a bloodclaate blind eye.

No wonder the world is fucked because what they should see they refuse to see.

Refuse to help the children of Jamaica.

It seems you tongue must be in their assholes before they will help a black child. Hence I say fuck them because there is no justice in them. They're fucking assholes that see the ills of Babylon and fund them but when black children are being slaughtered like animals they turn a blind eye.

Now tell me world where is the justice in this world?

Where is the fucking equality?

Hence I get mad at the black communities of this world because we are fucking kiss asses that still have the fucked up and jacked up bloodclaate slave mentality. **_Fuck slavery and the black society because we seek to follow the fucking Babylonians instead of breaking away from them and develop a positive and progressive system and society for ourselves._**

We were never slaves nor did God – Good God make us slaves. We gave up our rights and now look at us. Gobbling up garbage that take away from our rich ancestry and being watered down and sold back to us.

We are all fucking morons that Good God cannot trust because we fucked up our history and incorporate fucking Babylon culture in ours without knowing it.

Yes I am angry because children are being molested daily in Jamaica and the stinking worse than gutta belly, stink bad worse than the demons of hell government in Jamaica refuse to do something about this.

Trust me God – Good God is not sleeping and I will not chant a psalm for them. I know for a fact their hell hole in hell will be hotter than death. This I promise and give you my word on. *If I have to petition death directly to make their hell that hot and brutal I will just to make sure the children of Jamaica can live in peace and safety. Enough is enough man come on now.*

No wonder some people don't want to be fucking black because some of the shit our leaders do to our own not only sickens humanity but LITERALLY SICKENS GOD – GOOD GOD himself.

We are a fucking disgrace when it comes to the banner of black. Hence it repented God – Good God to make man because of the shit we do to self and our children.

But trust me hell is there for some and their children – family. *Trust me I give you the world my word that Good God will hear it from me when it comes to the children of this world. He will have to answer for this because forgiveness goes both ways and I swear by my life that if I can charge him Good God for child* _abandonment in his own court and courts of justice I will._

No child should be raped and slaughtered by grown ass man including women.

No I am fucking mad at God - Good God because he sees this shit happening and turn a fucking blind eye to it. How the fuck can we trust him to have our backs when he can't protect our children from shit like this? Scum bags that think this is okay.

I know some parents are to blame because some of them sell their children to the highest bidder. But I still blame God because he caused gutta belly sewage rats that call themselves mothers to have children when he should have made them fucking barren.

Nothing can wane my anger right now because it's not right for grown ass mother***ing pricks to be sleeping with children.

Demarco's song is not wrong because this is what many of us grow up in hence we carry on this nasty and stinking tradition.

This is also what the bible teaches hence we carry on with the nasty and stinking traditions of the worthless book of nastiness called the holy bible. But the children of God know better that the bible is called the book of sin. The holy bible is sins book. The book that billions to hell – their deaths.

We talk about church and God and the same fucking scum bags that are called pastors are raping people of their dignity then a pree God.

Hence I ask what religion is God because I truly do not want to be a part of God's whoring and stinking society – system of things because he upholds nastiness hence he's fucking nasty.

This is life and like I said, true love does not hurt and in all I see, I see an unjust God that let evil and wicked people dominate and control and refuses to do anything about it.

No people I am mad because who feels it knows it. Hence I say Good God is not fair when it comes to humanity because he permits this - slackness. He can stop this. He can because he can shut down evil meaning return evil to sender and he will not interfere.

Yes I know we as parents choose evil but the children are innocent man. They are innocent and it's not right for us to neglect our children. We have to stop fucking them up and teach them right.

They (our children) have a future and we as adults are fucking them up. Hence fuck the BABYLONIAN WAY OF LIFE because Bob Marley was right when he said Jah would never give his power to a bald head. And the Babylonians are fucking bald heads that could never ever possess the BREATH OF LIFE.

God – Good God would never ever, infinitely never ever give them his life – breath which is Allelujah. Hence they rob the NAME ALLAH FROM ALLELUJAH. They cannot say Allelujah because they are not a part of Good God's kingdom and master plan. They are the fucking devil's own hence the devil run the fucking world because of their evils and lies. Especially their lying book called the bible which is the book of sin. A stinking book of lies they feed humanity – the people of the world to bring your asses to hell with them and you gobble

up their fucking bullshit like dumb asses.

There is life and death hence the Star of David or Mogen David which is the marrying of life with death. When you marry the triangle it means you're fucking going to die. You're hell bound. This was what Eve did. She married death hence she frigging died.

Good are never to marry evil because when good marries evil, evil is born. This is what Eve did hence Cain killed Abel. She married evil and there are no ands ifs or buts about this. This according to your book of sin but I've told you the true truth in my other books.

Yes I know I am venting and you are to ask Good God for good and true children before we have them but I cannot knowing condone the shit that is happening in Jamaica. How much more children should be slaughtered like pigs in the country for the world take notice? One death is too many. All we can do is sing. Fucking do something like commission the fucking international community to do something and hold the Jamaican Government fucking accountable for these crimes.

Both the JLP and PNP should be prosecuted for these crimes because the slaughtering and raping of children have been going on for decades. And none of you better bring the book of sin into this because I know about the nastiness of Lot and his daughter including Abraham and Sarah, Nimrod and his mother. Family banging or having sex with each other hence royalty and family rams. Ramkoran, hence the Koran or Quran of the nasty and stinking Babylonians.

Good God would never condone this nastiness. I know this for an infinite and indefinite fact. **_If masturbation is a fucking sin what makes shagging your family member holy?_** It's not holy. It's a fucking sin and everyone knows this but in Babylonian culture and society this is lawful hence there are no Babylonians in Good God's kingdom. **_Hence Sud and Nod were separate and apart and the strife between Good God's children and the devil's own (children)._**

The children of God – Good God were not to mingle or marry the children of Nod because they were that filthy and nasty. Eve knew about their nastiness hence she broke the code and listened to them hence filth now dominates the world.

They got their way into God's garden but could never ever get into Good God's kingdom.

Man I am mad and on this note I am going to end this book because if I continue on I will become more severe and I truly don't want to do that today.

Yes it's my day and I have to leave things here.

Hence I ask you this Good God. How can you love us so and see the injustices of children globally and do nothing to help them? Yes I know these books but see with me now.

How can you love us so and turn a blind eye to what's happening in this world?

How can you love us so and continually allow grown ass men and women to rape children? Yes I know many of us grow up in this nastiness thinking it is okay but you know it is not okay. We need to change us Good God and you are the key to this change. Like I've told you time and time again, the full truth must be known. Evil has screwed up humanity with its nasty book called the holy bible and you can no longer stand aside and look.

You cannot let evil continue to send humanity to hell thinking the nasty book of sin called the bible or holy bible is lawful – good. You know the bible is sins book and it's time you shut sin the hell down and let humanity live free and clean.

You cannot say you love us so and watch us die. Come on now.

Like I said, loving us so in not loving us true hence I question the validity of you loving us so.

How can you love us so when we are screwing up our children's future?

How can you say you love us so and stand aside and look while evil – evil people in this world ruin the lives of others?

How can you say you love us so and allow sin to ravish the people of earth by continually feeding us lies to eat drink and die?

How can you love us so when evil spread each and every day and nothing is being done on your part to put a stop to the evil of the lands – earth? Evil is real Good God and you know it and you cannot abandon us. We deserve the truth. We deserve the right to choose for ourselves and not have someone choose for us.

You know that evil does not play on a level playing field and you have no right to condone this. Life is life and not evil because you gave us good life all around and it is not fair for evil to take good life from us.

Tell me something Good God who is the guilty one now?

You have the ability to help so help because not everyone is far gone. You can save the righteous so do it. No child should be subjected to abuse of grown ass men preying on them.

If they these men and women are going to prey on children let their dicks fall off or be damn well castrated. Women should their vagina sewed up if they continually do shit like this. Come on now. Who the hell are we to screw up a child's life without remorse?

This was originally done hence genital mutilation. Men had their dicks cut off and women had their vagina mutilated.

The Babylonians of modern day do this act in reverse. You know this so what is stopping you from doing this today? Your law and laws have not changed. Do right now man come on now.

Like I said Good God, you are to blame because you created negative energy and you knew the chaos it would cause if left to fester – spread. You are not innocent in all of this because evil could have been stopped a long time ago but you had to give them time.

You Good God had nothing to prove to evil hence you should not have given evil time to deceive. You were wrong in doing so because you knew how vile sin is. Now look at the vile acts of sin humanity commit in your sight on a daily basis.

No Good God today is my day and I am not holding back. I don't care if you don't like me anymore as long as you truly love me. Like I've said, I can't be dishonest with you. I have to be honest hence I am this way with you. Yes you are God – Good God and I have a right to blame you for certain things because evil and or sin was not necessary.

No form of sin is necessary and it matters not about will- the choice we make as humans. Sin had no right to do this and you know it.

Yes sin has no rules when it comes to sacrificing humanity to death. That's sins job and he must do it hence we are accountable for our sins – wrongs.

I truly love you but the mess of earth has to stop. Like I said, let death take his people and be gone and truly leave your people alone. We do not have to witness nor see the acts of sin. We have rights too and sin is not our right you are. Come on now.

Let death take his people so that we can be infinitely and indefinitely be rid of them so we can live good, true and clean forever ever in you and with you.

I need this Good God because I don't know how much more I can take. Hence I tell you I am holding you responsible for sin and death – negative energy. Negative energy should not feed off positive energy hence death's children should not feed off the Breath of Life – your good and true children including you.

You are our right. You are our children's right and if our children are screwed up, how can they be any good to you?

God – Good God when we are screwed up, will we not raise screwed up children?

Now tell me this. When these children grow up to say there is no God or they hate you what do you say?

When they (these children) say they hate you because you abandoned them, were not there for them what say you?

Look into yourself now Good God and truly tell me if you can blame them for saying they hate you?

Can you hold them guilty because in truth you were not there for them? They felt the pain and hurt. They were the ones to feel hate, feel unloved, neglected. They felt the abuse. They were looking to you for protection, a saving grace and hope and you were truly not there.

So tell me now, how could you have loved us so?

No Good God, I am not against you and will never be against you but you also have to face reality. No one want to hurt and feel pain and under this current global system it hurts and we feel pain.

It's like I keep telling you about me being held captive in a land that I do not want to be in and you are not listening to me. I'm not the only one that feel this way.

**Like I said, I more than infinitely truly love you as well as share your pain because I know your tears. But we are hurting too. No one should take you and your truth from us. You are my right – our right and I am reclaiming you hence truly do right by me and your people because I more than desire you and your goodness and truth.**

You have hope and true love in me so take it and save your people. I know I am hardnosed with you but you made me this way. If I can't be true and honest as well as clean with you what good am I to you and your people?

Michelle Jean